Hog-Killing Time

Millie Jean Coppedge

RonJon Publishing, Inc.

10-05-'05

Jane,

Enjoy your "walk" back into my childhood.

Millie Jean

This book is dedicated to my children Wendy Lynn Murphy and Donald Franklin Pearce, Jr.

"May I leave this small piece of memories of my childhood that you may know some of the events that occurred which helped build my character."

In Memory of:

Barney, my Daddy, Bruce Olen, my brother, and both sets of grandparents,
Lydia and Alvie Coppedge and
Alfred and Lillie Mae Reed.

In Appreciation to:

Bill Anderson, Longview, Texas
Who so painstakingly edited my manuscript.

Hog-Killing Time

1954

October 4, 1954—Monday

My name is Millie Jean Coppedge and I am 8 years old. I had my first birthday party Saturday and this pretty blue diary is one of the things that I got as a present. Mother invited all ten kids in my class and a few other special friends, but only five and their mothers came. But it didn't matter. We had lots of fun. Mother said we were going to have my party on Saturday so people would be free to come, especially since she wanted all the mothers to get to know each other. A weekday is not a good day for some people.

We played games like *Pin the Tail on the Donkey*, ate cake and ice cream, then went outside and played games, while the mothers talked.

I got a pink wallet, some new shoes and blue jeans, some play makeup, and several other things, but this diary is my favorite. Margaret gave it to me. She is one of my favorite friends.

October 6, 1954—Wednesday

Today I got to wear the new blue jeans my mother and daddy gave me for my birthday. They are bright red, blue, yellow, and green stripped flannel inside and are so warm. Mother rolled up the cuffs like all the other kids, and I wore my new shoes. I wanted some penny loafers, the kind you put a shiny new penny in the slot, but everyone in my grade wears lace up oxfords, so that is what I got. Janie Sue, a girl who rides my bus and is in the 9th grade, wears penny loafers. Mother says I'm not old enough yet. I love writing in my diary. I can say secret things, and no one can read it but me.

October 7, 1954—Thursday

I need to tell you that we live on a farm. We have cows, pigs, chickens, and a plow horse named Jake. Daddy milks the two cows every morning before he goes to work and then again at night. Mother takes care of preparing the fresh milk. Daddy also gathers the eggs. Late in the evening after supper, Bruce, my little brother, and I help feed the hogs. Bruce is only four and he doesn't go to school yet.

On our back porch by the well-house, is a big five gallon bucket where we rake all our scraps of left over food. Things like pea shells, corn husks, etc. also go in the bucket. Then, Daddy stirs a little pig food like corn or shorts in with the scraps and we pour it into the pig trough. I especially love to feed the pigs.

They snort and root, and gobble down the food in no time. They get it all over themselves, from their ears to their tails, sometimes even in their eyes.

Most people think pigs really stink, but I don't. I like to smell them. Just like with the baby chickens, we really get attached to them. When you feed, talk to, and play with animals every day, they become your friends. It's so hard to think about the fact that someday you will be eating them. I don't want to be a farmer when I grow up. I don't know yet what I want to be, but it's not a farmer! I don't mind helping Daddy milk the cows, but I wouldn't want to have to do it every day of my life, especially in the frigid wintertime.

Grandmother Reed has to milk seven or eight cows every morning and every evening all by herself. She doesn't wear pants, says a lady doesn't wear pants. So, on the horrible winter days, she is out there in her cow pen milking with just a cotton dress and a heavy coat on. I feel so sorry for her. Like I said: I do not want to be a farmer! No sire!

October 9, 1954—Saturday

It has been raining for three days. The red clay road we live on is so slippery that Daddy's car slid into the ditch on the way to work this morning. A log truck pulled him out with a big heavy chain. We live in the country not far from the sawmill, where they cut lumber, the kind used to build houses. Pulpwood trucks go by our house all day long, loaded with long, heavy logs to be cut at the mill. Once the trucks are unloaded, they go back by empty, headed for the woods to haul out more trees. When the dirt road is dry, heavy waves of dust fly from the trucks and coat our house, car, and us, if we are out there. But for now, I'm tired of the rain.

October 10, 1954—Sunday

Bad day! Very bad day! It's still raining. Snowball, our white Collie, likes to chase cars. Daddy has spanked him many times trying to break him from chasing them, but he keeps on doing it.

This morning, we were eating breakfast. We heard one of the pulpwood trucks coming and the driver started blowing his horn really loud and long. We all got up and ran out onto the back porch in time to see Snowball running along beside the truck's front wheels. Suddenly, Snowball slipped and fell under the front tire, and the truck ran over him. The driver stopped and Daddy ran down the road toward the truck. I've never seen Daddy run before. I was so scared.

We saw Daddy walking back down the middle of the muddy road carrying Snowball in his arms like a baby. He trudged up the driveway, then gently laid him in the front yard. Our solid white Collie was totally red, partly from the red mud, partly from blood. Daddy cried and cried. That was the first time I've ever seen my daddy cry.

Daddy buried Snowball in the woods behind our house. He was gone a long time. I guess he was crying some more. Poor Daddy. He loved Snowball so much. Every morning when Daddy would get in the car to leave for work, Snowball always jumped up and wanted to go with him, and in the evening when he got back home, Snowball would be waiting at the front of the driveway. He would jump all over Daddy until Daddy would finally stop and play with him. Sad, sad day.

October 15, 1954—Friday

It sure is lonely without Snowball. We all miss him, but Daddy really loved him a lot. Daddy just sits out on the back porch every evening after he comes in from work. He works at Uncle Raymond's garage. He sits there until Mother calls him for supper, then afterwards goes back out and sits there until way after dark. I keep thinking Snowball will come running around from the back of the house, or that I'll look down the road and see him beating it toward the house.

Tomorrow we are going to the Yamboree. We go every year. It is held in Gilmer from Wednesday until Saturday. I'll tell you more about it after we get back tomorrow night.

October 17, 1954—Sunday

Well, we got in too late last night from the Yamboree for me to write about it. Boy, I am still tired this morning! We got up early yesterday and had a big breakfast—pancakes, bacon and eggs. Mother says that she doesn't want us getting hungry too early. She packed us some sandwiches, fried peach pies, and a jug of ice tea for lunch. Most people bring a lunch as the food at the Yamboree is so expensive and tastes like old grease.

Oh, a Yamboree is a country fair. It is called Yamboree because it started with all the farmers bringing their garden-grown fruits and vegetables to town like a market for everyone to buy or trade. They also brought their livestock to enter in contests or auction off. Eventually it developed into a fair-like atmosphere with all types of rides like the roller coaster, Ferris wheel, merry-go-round, and many more. All types of arcade games like pick-up-the-ducks, and shoot the balloon, line one whole side of the street around the courthouse. The smell of hot dogs, waffle cakes, cotton candy, candied apples, and many more wonderful, delicious foods fill the air.

We got there about eight o'clock in the morning. At first we just walked around looking at everything, seeing what rides were there this year and if there were any new games in the arcade. We talked to a lot of old friends and relatives. I saw a lot of the kids from school.

About eight forty-five we lined up in front of the court house along with several hundred other people, getting ready to see the parade. At nine, the fire truck could be heard with its siren blaring from several blocks away. That was everyone's clue that the parade was starting.

Daddies put their kids on top of their shoulders so they could see over the crowd. Mothers held onto the little ones' hands to keep them from darting out into the path of the parade. I love the parade. There are a lot of bands, brightly decorated floats, people parading new and very old cars, people in all types of costumes, clowns, and at the very end are about 50 -100 horses ridden by kids, women and men.

After the parade, Mother and Daddy let Bruce and me wander around on our own. That's the best part of the day! We can watch people on the rides and listen to the carnival music. Weeks before the Yamboree was to come to town, Bruce and I did a lot of odd jobs to make a little spending money. We only had $2 each and it's really hard to decide what to spend it on. We talked about the rides we wanted to go on and what we wanted to eat. I always like the pink cotton candy and Bruce likes the caramel apples. We like the red roller coaster and Ferris wheel. Rides are ten cents each.

Bruce tried to win a blue teddy bear by throwing darts at balloons, but he missed every time. The man gave him a yellow whistle for trying. I didn't want to gamble my money away. I would rather eat something, so I got a fried waffle that the lady had just taken out of the grease vat. She sprinkled white powdered sugar all over it from a flour sifter. I ate the whole thing all by myself. It was so good. But I belched rancid, stale grease the rest of the day. Next year maybe I'll get the caramel apple.

After sundown, the whole town square was lit up with colored lights on the rides and throughout the arcade. The Yamboree is much more fun at night. Most time, we wait until after dark to ride the Ferris wheel, so we can see all the town's bright lights. It's like being in a space ship about to land in the unsuspecting town.

At 10:00 P.M., the rides all quit, the arcade began to take down their tents, and everything shut down. The Yamboree was over until again next year, and the crowd headed for their cars. Bruce and I slept all the way home, about sixteen miles. The next morning Daddy found blisters on Bruce's feet from the new shoes he was wearing. Bruce never even said a thing about his feet hurting at the Yamboree. I guess he was just too excited to notice.

October 18, 1954—Monday

Last night I had a terrible dream, but it was about a thing that really happened when I was almost five. Bruce was a tiny baby then. We lived in the town part of Ore City, although only two stores, a garage, two filling stations and a café made up the entire town.

We were renting a house on the main highway. About daylight one morning, Mother says it was six o'clock, the teenaged boy next door went out to burn the trash. His house and ours were owned by the same man, and we shared a barrel in the middle of the backyard on the property line for the purpose of burning our trash. The boy poured gasoline on the trash to get the fire started.The wind was high, and the fire got out of control and caught the grass on fire. It quickly spread to our house, then to theirs. Our town was so tiny, there was no fire department. Our only source of water was wells, so trying to put out the fires was fruitless. With the wind so high, both our houses burned like an old wood pile. Mother and Daddy saved very little of our stuff. Even Bruce's and my baby pictures disintegrated into ashes. I dream of the fire often and worry that our new house will burn down, too.

After the fire, the town got together and built a shell of a house for us to live in. Granddaddy Coppedge gave us five acres of land on his place. One weekend the townspeople turned out and all came to work. The saw mill donated the lumber, a store in town donated the nails and sheetrock, etc. In just one weekend, they built a shell of a house for us to live in.

The front part of the house was eventually completed, with linoleum floors and Venetian blinds. Mother and Daddy work a little at a time as we got the extra money, but the kitchen still doesn't have running water, so we have to boil water on the cook stove to wash dishes and take a bath. We don't have any plumbing at all to the house, thus, no bathroom. We take our baths on the back porch in a number three washtub.

In the winter, we take our baths in the kitchen. It is more fun bathing on the porch because we bathe by moonlight, so people driving down the road won't see us. Even though we call the porch our back porch, it is really on the side of the house, visible from the road. Of course, down that long dirt road, not many people pass after dark. The colored people who work at the saw mill are the only ones who live down below us, and they walk everywhere they go. They don't usually go anywhere after dark.

We use the outdoor toilet at the edge of the woods behind the house and at night have a Mrs. Tucker's Shortening can under the edge of both beds to pee in. If we have to do the "big job" during the night, we have to go outside and around behind the house. In the winter, it is really cold. It is always my job to empty both "cans" as we call them. I draw a little water from the well, rinse the cans, and hang them on the fence post to dry and air out. It doesn't take long for the cans to begin to rust with all that urine sitting in them all night, so every time Mother empties another can, we throw the rusty one away and use the new one. Once the cans rust, they stink really bad.

We don't have linoleum, blinds, or curtains for the back of the house yet. We haven't gotten a sink or commode for the bathroom. Daddy did buy a used tub, but since we don't have running water, it's used for storage. The whole bathroom itself is used to store Christmas decorations, blankets, and stuff we don't use very often.

October 29, 1954—Friday

It's just two days until Halloween. It sure is cold for trick-or-treating, but we'll just bundle up real good.

This week, our teacher Miss Beverly decorated the classroom with pumpkins, witches and ghosts that she had cut out of construction paper. We all got to draw scary or funny Halloween pictures and she thumb-tacked them all around the room.

Today Beth's mother brought orange and black cupcakes for a snack after lunch. Beth said she helped her decorate them last night. I really like cupcakes. Miss Beverly told us scary stories after our snack. She turned out the lights and lit candles. That was my favorite part of the day.

The worst part of the day was when I was drinking my second cup of punch. I was drinking it too fast and sucked a big piece of the ice down my throat. It hung in my throat.

Though I coughed and coughed, I couldn't get it to come up and though I swallowed hard, it wouldn't go on down. It was so cold my head was throbbing, and I was really scared. The kids gathered around me and just watched. I guess they didn't know what to do. Someone yelled for Miss Beverly and she ran over and hit me real hard in the back with the flat part of her hand. The ice flew out of my throat and clear across the room. Miss Beverly saved my life. I could have choked to death. I will sure be more careful next time I drink punch or **anything** with ice in it.

October 31, 1954—Sunday

Today is Halloween! Mother dressed Bruce and me like hobos. We can't afford to buy a fancy costume like the ones they sell at Mrs. Virginia's store. Mother burned several matches and used the soot to smear over our faces to make us look like hobos. She tied a colorful rag from her sewing scrap bag, around our heads, like gypsies. Daddy got us each a tall stick to carry, "just for looks" he said. That means to make us look more like hobos.

We drove into town, and Mother and Daddy let us get out at kinfolks houses and people we know to trick-or treat. Then, we drove to Grandmother and

Granddaddy Reed's. She always gives us extra-special stuff that she doesn't give every body else. She gave us popcorn balls fresh out of the pot, still warm. She makes the best, buttery ones. They just melt in your mouth. She also gave us some peanut butter cookies and a nickel.

Last, we stopped by Grandmother and Granddaddy Coppedge's. She had made brownies, and they too gave us money. They gave us each five shiny new pennies. Granddaddy gets them at the bank to give on Halloween and Christmas. Bruce and I love new money.

We had a nice bag of candy by the time we got home about 9 o'clock. Mother let us eat the popcorn ball and the brownie, but said we would have to wait until tomorrow to eat any more as it was time to go to bed, and she didn't want us to have nightmares from going to bed with a lot of junk in our stomachs.

November 1, 1954—Monday

The sky started to turn really dark. After supper, the wind blew hard and it started to rain by the buckets. A big, heavy boom of thunder hit, and all the lights in the house went out. In a few seconds, pieces of golf ball size hail started coming through the two front living room windows. We have a double bed in our living room instead of a couch. It sits right under the front windows. The bed was too low for us to get under, so Mother grabbed a quilt from the hall closet and threw it over us as we huddled on the floor all squeezed together. When the glass started flying across the bed with such force that some of it hit the opposite wall, Daddy jumped up and grabbed the bedspread and quilt that were on the bed, stood up in the middle of the bed, and held them over the window to try to keep the pouring rain and hail out. It was a good thing Daddy had his shoes on. He always pulls his shoes off at the back door and goes barefooted in the house. We could hear the glass crunching beneath his feet. He had to hold the covers up for a really long time. It was so dark. Bruce and I were mighty scared.

But finally the storm stopped, Mother and Daddy cleaned up the water and glass, and Daddy went to get a piece of wood from behind the smokehouse to put over the windows until he could fix them. A scary day!

November 2, 1954—Tuesday

Daddy brought home some glass and fixed the windows. It took him three hours to completely clean out the old glass and dried-out putty and put in the new panes.

November 6, 1954—Saturday

About ten o'clock this morning, Aunt Patti, Uncle Hollis, their two boys and Grandmother and Granddaddy Reed came to visit. These grandparents are my mother's parents. Aunt Patti and Uncle Hollis had just gotten back from Michigan where Aunt Patti's folks live. They brought a big batch of fish that they had caught while they were there. All the women worked in the kitchen cooking dinner while the men sat on the back porch and talked. We had fried fish, soft-fried potatoes with onions, green beans, a big salad, hot biscuits and chocolate pie.

The strangest thing about those fish was that you could eat the whole thing, bones and all. Of course the head was cut off and the guts taken out, like any other fish, but Uncle Hollis said this was a special kind of fish that they have in Michigan, and he wanted to share them with us. It seemed so strange to bite into the whole fish like a donut, chew it up and swallow the whole thing. The bones just dissolved in our mouths. They were really good.

November 15, 1954—Monday

Tomorrow the county nurse, Mrs. Clayton, is coming to give everyone their booster shots. I hate those stupid old shots. The needle is really long and leaves a hole in your arm for days. We have to have a booster shot every year that we are in elementary school. Maybe I'll wake up sick and won't have to go to school tomorrow. I bet I don't sleep all night worrying about it.

November 16, 1954—Tuesday

I think the needles were bigger this year than ever. Mary Jo cried at just seeing them. A lot of kids cried, even some of the big sixth graders. Mrs. Clayton is so sweet and smiles all the time, but I wish she weren't our nurse. I'd rather she cooked in the cafeteria with Mrs. Hudspeth. She loves all the kids and sometimes, she gives us free cookies.

While we were all in line for the shots, I could smell the hot rolls and red beans Mrs. Hudspeth was cooking in the lunch room. Every day the smell of whatever she is cooking begins to fill our classrooms about nine o'clock, and by lunch time, I'm starved. Today, I could hardly raise my arm to eat, it hurt so bad from the shot. Everyone was quiet at lunch. In fact, we were quiet the rest of the day.

November 17, 1954—Wednesday

Mother gave me some aspirin last night so I could sleep. My arm was really aching by supper time. This morning it hurts even worse. There is a really big knot, and it's red and hot. Mother put an icepack on it while I ate breakfast, but it didn't help any. I couldn't even comb my hair because I couldn't raise my arm. Mother had to comb my hair and put the barrettes in. When I got on the bus, everyone was still quiet. Everyone had the same sore arm. A few kids had to stay home because they had such high fevers. I'll be glad when I'm grown and don't have to take those stupid shots any more.

November 20, 1954—Saturday

It's been over a month since Snowball got killed. Daddy sure is sad without him. Snowball would follow Daddy everywhere he went, and when Daddy sat down on the back porch to pull off his old work boots at the end of the day, Snowball would lay snug against him and whine. The whine was Snowballs way of telling Daddy to pet him. Daddy would sit and rub him and talk to him softly. I asked Daddy if we could get another dog but he said no. He doesn't want to get attached to another one. He said this road is just too dangerous with all the log trucks flying by all day long. He said he even worries about one of us kids getting hurt, and he told us not to play in the ditch anymore. I guess he just wasn't thinking, because we have never been allowed to play in the ditch.

November 21, 1954—Sunday

Grandmother and Granddaddy Coppedge, Daddy's parents, live just across the field from us. Early this morning, Daddy's sister Aunt Mildred, her husband, Uncle Audrey, their son Ralph, Aunt Zelma, Daddy's other sister, Uncle Jim, her husband and their two kids, Jimmy and June, came to Grandmother's to spend the day. We walked across the pasture to go visit. Mother took a banana pudding and some purple hull peas.

We had a big dinner and I even got to eat in the dining room with the adults. The rest of the kids had to eat in the kitchen on the red and white metal table.

It's a special treat to eat at Grandmother Coppedge's. She let me take the white linen table cloth and napkins out of her buffet and set the table. She insisted that I put the pad under the tablecloth so the dark shiny finish on her table wouldn't get scratched or ruined. I don't like the pad because the ice tea glasses won't set flat. They wobble. It makes me nervous and I am always afraid that my glass will turn over, and tea will soak up into her pretty tablecloth.

Today everything went great. I got to eat and talk with the adults like I was really somebody special. After dinner, Grandmother Coppedge played the piano and June and I sang, while everyone spread all over the house to talk. I love to hear Grandmother play. She and Granddaddy travel all over the countryside to all day singings and "dinner on the ground". Grandmother plays the piano while Granddaddy leads the singing for special songs he has chosen. The people at the singings take turns leading everyone in their favorite songs. Boy, can Granddaddy sing! His deep voice booms across the tops of everyone's head, keeping them in tune.

When Aunt Zelma comes to visit, she always brings us a box of clothes that her family has outgrown. Before they left, she went to her car and brought in **two boxes** this time. I could hardly wait until I got home to see what she brought.

About four o'clock, they left headed back home to Dallas. Aunt Mildred stayed a while, then they left. Mother and Daddy took the boxes and we headed across the field toward home.

"Walk fast!" I told Daddy. "I want to see what Aunt Zelma brought!"

Well, this was the best stuff we've ever gotten. She had also brought some things that Aunt Jetty and Uncle Roy sent. They also live in Dallas and he is Granddaddy's brother. Granddaddy Coppedge was the twenty first of twenty two children. I can't imagine that! A family having twenty two kids! **Wow!** Anyway, the boxes were crammed full of good stuff. There was a real leather purse with engraved designs all over it for a girl just my age. It had been June's, but it looked like new. June is older than me and doesn't carry a kiddy purse any more.We got toboggans, shoes and belts. I got a yellow and an orange sweater. Bruce doesn't get much because Jimmy is so much older than Bruce, and it would be years before he could wear the clothes. I think they give Jimmy's to someone else. Sometimes he can wear some of June's jeans and shirts around the house for play. Daddy and Mother get a few things, but mostly I get stuff. I'm going to carry my new purse to school tomorrow and show Margaret. She doesn't have a purse. Maybe I'll give her my old one. It's still pretty.

November 22, 1954—Monday

Oh, I forgot to tell you about the best thing in the boxes besides the purse. On the very bottom of the second box was a pair of roller skates. We've never had roller skates before. The good thing is that they are adjustable, so they will fit Bruce **and** me. There are little screws that you turn to make them longer or shorter. On the side, (right where Grandmother Coppedge's bunions are on her feet), is a part that screws in or out to make the skates tighten or loosen on your feet according to what size your feet are.

There is a skate key that we use to tighten or loosen them. Since we live in the country and don't have a sidewalk like city folks do, there is no place to skate. Daddy said Bruce and I could skate across the back of the house. We can skate from their bedroom, through the long hall, and to the end of the other bedroom. The front of the house has linoleum rugs, but the back of the house only has wood floors. They're perfect for skating. It's just like the city skating rink floor, Daddy says.

We love the skates. Bruce skates while I'm at school, since he doesn't go to school yet. Then I can skate when I get home. We both have to hold onto the wall, but Daddy says it won't be long before we can fly down the hall without holding onto anything. Mother doesn't mind because the skates don't leave marks on the floor. Even if they did, it wouldn't matter. Someday we are going to put linoleum on the back floors like the front of the house.

November 30, 1954—Tuesday

Tonight the electricity went out again. Daddy got the coal oil lamps down from the loft. Mother was right in the middle of cooking something on the cook stove and she told him to hurry up and get one lit. She wouldn't let us come in the kitchen. She said that it was a surprise. I noticed that she had buttered a long glass dish and left it on the dinning room table, and from the smell drifting through the house, it smelled like candy. Holding the heavy iron skillet with two hot pads, she came in and poured a skillet full of something bubbly into the buttered dish. It smelled heavenly, and we had never had anything that looked like that before.

When it cooled, Mother cut it with a knife (in little pieces) like she does fudge. She gave Daddy a piece first to see the reaction on his face. He loved it and asked for another piece. After my first bite, I turned to Bruce and told him that this was the best stuff I'd ever tasted. He quickly gobbled his down almost choking on every bite, then hurriedly asked for more.

"What is this?" Daddy asked.

"It's peanut candy. I made up the recipe out of my head," Mother said. First I parched a batch of peanuts we had drying in the smokehouse, while ya'll were milking the cows. The smell of supper cooking after that took away all the smell of the peanuts, so you wouldn't be suspicious that I was up to something. I wanted it to be a surprise. Then I mixed molasses and a few other ingredients, added the peanuts, and slow cooked it on the cook stove. I didn't know how it would turn out, but it sure is good," Mother said with a big smile.

December 1, 1954—Wednesday

While I was at school today, Grandmother Coppedge got really sick, and Granddaddy had to take her to Gilmer to the hospital. The doctor said she had a heart attack. Mother and Daddy followed Granddaddy to the hospital and stayed there all day, until time for my bus to get home. Then we all went to Gilmer again. They won't let me see Grandmother. Only the adults can go into her room. Bruce and I had to sit out in the waiting room with some people we didn't even know. They looked out for us.

It was real late when we got home. They are really worried about Grandmother. I'm so scared. I want to cry, but the big lump in my throat just won't let me. It feels like my heart is crying, though. The doctor said that they would know in a day or two if she will "pull through". That means if she will live or not. I heard Mother and Daddy talking about it all the way home. They thought we were asleep in the back seat because Bruce was snoring so loud. But I heard them talk all the way home. Daddy is really worried about his mother. She had never been sick before.

December 3, 1954—Friday

This afternoon when I got off the bus, Mother said that Grandmother was going to be all right. She may be home soon, and will would have to have peace and quiet and take a lot of expensive heart medicine. Grandmother and Granddaddy don't have much money. I think they're worried about how much the medicine will cost. Maybe we can give them some money. Daddy says we don't have much money, either.

December 9, 1954—Thursday

Late this evening just before dark, I really got into trouble. Margaret is my best friend. In fact, most times, she is my only friend. On Thursdays and Fridays, we get to take a toy to school to play with at recess time. It's really cold outside, but we don't care. At recess, Margaret and I went way out to the edge of the woods and played in our secret place behind the big tree. Our school is a really small country school. We even have to go to the edge of the woods to use the outhouse. The drinking fountain is outside next to the school building by the big cedar trees.

Well, back to my story. Margaret and I were playing house with our dolls and we decided on a plan. After school, I would come home with her to play. She has a lot of dolls at her house, and said that we could play in her playhouse in her back yard. All afternoon we were so excited we could hardly stand the wait.

The bus always goes by her house before mine, so I just got off at her house. She introduced me to her mother and daddy then we went to her room to look at the dolls. Her daddy is in a wheelchair. He works at home repairing watches. Her Mother doesn't work. She just takes care of Margaret's daddy.

After a few minutes, we took the dolls and went into the back yard to her playhouse. It was really neat. Her uncle built it underneath a tall sweet gum tree, and it was just like a little miniature house. We were having so much fun when Margaret's mother brought us some cookies and milk. What could have been more perfect?

"This is the most fun I've ever had", I told her mother, and thanked her for the snack. As the afternoon went on, we put the dolls away and went out in the front yard. We were talking to the man who lived next door when my mother drove up in Margaret's driveway. She looked really mad. I didn't know what was wrong. She was really upset that I hadn't come home on the bus.

She told Margaret's mother and daddy that when the bus passed our house and didn't stop to let me off, she got scared. She waited for the bus to turn around and come back down the road, then flagged him down. The bus driver told her that he had let me off at Margaret's house. When Daddy got home with the car, (we only have one car) she came over there to get me.

Boy, was I in trouble! But I didn't think it would be wrong to go play for a little while. I didn't even think about Mama and Daddy not knowing where I was. In fact, I didn't even think about going home or how I would get there. All I thought about was going to Margaret's house to play. I had never been to the house of a classmate to play before.

December 10, 1954—Friday

Yesterday when Margaret and I were playing in the front yard, we watched Mr. Edmondson's monkey playing. I had never seen a real live monkey before. It is chained to a dog house in the shade under a tree in the front yard. Margaret says that, at night, Mr. Edmondson takes him inside like a puppy so he will stay warm, and the wild animals like wolves won't hurt him.

Margaret's daddy said a monkey cost a lot of money. And they are real mean. The monkey is chained up because if someone comes to visit, the monkey, named Chips, might bite them. Once he broke the chain and was gone for three days before someone called Mr. Edmondson to say they saw him down by Quaver's River. Mr. Edmondson and a bunch of his friends took a big net, and they caught him while he was getting a drink from the river.

I wish I had a monkey for a pet. But I would want a baby one and for it to be gentle and not mean. But now, we can't even have a dog. We sure couldn't have a monkey! I can just imagine going home and asking Daddy for a pet monkey. He would probably laugh so hard he would fall off the porch.

Grandmother Coppedge came home today. She has lost a lot of weight and is shaky when she walks or tries to eat. She had to go straight to bed. She has to eat in bed and even has a pee pot underneath the bed for when she needs to use the bathroom. I sure am glad she's home. Everyone is. Granddaddy loves her so much. He'll take good care of her.

December 14, 1954—Tuesday

It's been four days since Grandmother came home from the hospital. She is so much better. She sits up on the couch in the living room and even tried to play the piano a little today. Mother takes her some food so Granddaddy won't have to cook so much. Granddaddy's not a very good cook, but he tries.

December 16, 1954—Thursday

Late this afternoon, Daddy went into the woods behind our house and was gone for about an hour. He came back dragging a cedar tree. He made a stand out of some boards from the wood pile (to hold it up), then brought it into the house. We put in it the corner of the living room in front of the door.

Every year when we put our Christmas tree up, we can't use the front door. With a double bed in the living room, there is no other place big enough to put the tree.

Daddy strung the one string of lights we have around the tree. Mother made some popcorn. We dyed it different colors using cake coloring. Using quilting thread, we all helped string the popcorn with a big needle, like beads, then gently wound the rope of popcorn around and around the tree. Daddy brought in a bucket of sweet gum balls from the tree in Grandmother and Granddaddy Coppedge's front yard. Bruce and I wrapped tiny pieces of used aluminum foil Mother had saved from cooking, around each sweet gum ball. Then, as Mother cut lengths of red and green crochet string, and tied the strings to the stems of the balls, Daddy tied them onto the limbs of the tree. The tree may not be fancy with all the store-bought trimmings, but it sure is beautiful to us.

Mother drew a star on a piece of cardboard that Daddy brought in from the storeroom. She cut it out, and Bruce and I covered it with aluminum foil. Daddy placed it in the top of the tree. Then, Mother pieced together some cotton she used for quilting and spread it under the tree. We don't have any presents yet to go under it, but we don't need any. The tree is beautiful, all by itself.

December 19, 1954—Sunday

Today we went to Grandmother and Granddaddy Reed's. That's Mother's mother and daddy. We go there quite often for Sunday dinner and stay all day. All of my aunts, uncles, and cousins bring food and spend the day. Even if we don't go, Grandmother Reed has a house full every Sunday. Some times neighbors or friends come for dinner. Every now and then, we all take food and go to their houses. I really like going to other peoples houses. The kids play outside, and most of them have dogs or kittens or something neat to play on or with. Mr. Clifford, Granddaddy Reed's friend, has an old tractor that he lets us play on. It hasn't run in years, so it's safe for kids to play on. I haven't written about going to Grandmother Reed's before because one Sunday is just like the other.

December 20, 1954—Monday

Until we got our new wringer washer and three tubs for rinsing our clothes in, Mother washed our clothes in a tub on a scrub board. She used lye soap she made from rendering the hog fat she collected on hog killing day. Lye soap dries her hands out, making then turn red and crack. Sometimes in the winter they even bleed. Mother puts a salve on them that really stinks, but it doesn't help much.

With the new washer, Daddy agreed that Mother could take it and the tubs to Grandmother Reed's house so she could use it, too. Grandmother has a deeper well than we do and won't have to worry about draining the well dry. So, every Wednesday, Mother and Bruce go to Grandmother Reed's to do the wash. When I'm out of school, like for holidays and the summer, I get to go. too. Mother and Grandmother hang the clothes on her line to dry. It takes all day. Then, they fold the clothes and pack them into cardboard boxes to bring home.

Another one of my jobs before we got the washing machine was to hang the wash on the barbed wire fence. The fence runs from the back of the chicken yard to the front of the road.

Every week, our clothes took up the whole fence. It's pretty easy hanging the clothes out, because all I have to do is lay them over the line, and the barbs on the wire holds them in place. Taking them down is another matter, especially on a windy day. The wind or even a soft breeze twists the clothes round and round the wire. I have to be very gentle taking them off. All of our clothes have holes in them where the barbed wire goes through. So do all my friend's clothes. Everybody has to hang their clothes on fences to dry. Now, we will have a real clothes line at Grandmother's house, and use those pretty plastic clothes pins she bought at the dime store. They just clip over the clothes and hold on to them.

Another bad thing about hanging our clothes so close to the road when the big pulpwood trucks, butane trucks, or just people's cars passed by, the red dust would blow all over the clothes. It was bad enough if they were dry, but if they were still wet, that red dust would turn to red mud and dry stiff on our clothes. Sometimes if it was too bad, we would have to wash the clothes all over again.

Oh, and another thing. In the winter, the clothes would freeze to the fence and we couldn't get them off. Most of the time, if we knew that it was going to be that cold, we would hang them all over the inside of the house. Daddy would tie tiny, white ropes, to nails from corner to corner of each room, and we hung the clothes on them, but it really made it damp and cold in the house.

While I'm writing about clothes, let me tell you the rest of the story. Before we hang out the things that will need to be ironed, we boil blue Faultless Starch on the stove, dip those things in the thick starch, then hang them out to dry. Then, the day before Mother is ready to iron, she spreads the pink, blanket that was Bruce's and mine when we were babies on the kitchen table. She gets a small pan of water and sprinkles the clothes to be ironed, one at a time, rolls each into a tight ball, then wraps the blanket tightly around them in a big bundle. She lets them sit over night to allow the moisture to penetrate throughout each piece. This makes the clothes easier to iron. That way she doesn't have to sprinkle each piece as she irons. It saves a lot of time. If she doesn't get all the ironing done, she simply puts the bundle into the ice box, if it's summer time, so the clothes won't sour.

I'm learning to iron, but I don't like it at all. I'm afraid I will burn dark spots or holes in the clothes. I'm also afraid of burning myself! The iron gets really hot. Eric, in my class, said that last year his mother burned her arm really bad. It got infected, and they had to put her in the hospital and do something called skin grafts on her arm. He said it really hurt.

December 22, 1954—Wednesday

Mother and I have been baking and making candy for days. Saturday is Christmas Day, and we always have enough food cooked up so that we don't have to cook the entire day, but can just eat and enjoy all the things people do on that day. Mother said she will bake the last ham in the smokehouse on Friday. We still don't have much under our tree but Mother and Daddy's gifts from Bruce and me are there. Last Saturday while we were in Gilmer, we got Mother a bottle of "Evening in Paris" perfume and Daddy some pink nylon socks. Daddy just loves the color pink. I know he will be surprised when he sees them.

December 24, 1954—Friday

Well, the ham is cooked, the fruit cake mixed, and Bruce and I can hardly wait for Santa to come tonight. After supper, we had mugs of hot cocoa with melted marshmallows on top. M-m-m so good. We listened to some Christmas programs on the radio. One program had a lot of Christmas songs and music. Time to go to bed. Good-night!

December 25, 1954—Saturday

Bruce and I jumped out of bed before the sun had even come up this morning. When our feet hit the cold plank floor, we were so excited that we didn't even feel how cold it really was. We ran to the living room and straight to the tree.

Hearing the commotion, Daddy got up and lit the heater in the living room. Mother plugged in the tree lights and we all sat on the floor around the tree to see what Santa had brought.

Bruce had seen a "colored" baby doll in the store in Gilmer on one of our trips to town and had asked if he could have one like it for Christmas. Yes, I know, boys don't usually play with dolls, but that was what he wanted, and that is what he got. It is about ten inches long and is made out of soft rubber. I got one just like it, but mine is a "white" baby doll. I didn't want a colored baby. They each came with a soft pink blanket, diaper, and a bottle to feed them. The water from the bottle goes into a tiny hole in their mouths, runs through their tummies, then out a tiny hole in their bottoms. A baby that really wets! It is so exciting! Mother had made some clothes for both of them out of her quilt scraps. I recognized the material, but Bruce didn't. He thought Santa, or Mrs. Santa, made the clothes.

Bruce also got a red metal fire truck that makes a loud siren noise. It runs on batteries. I got some play make-up. We each got a snuff sack filled with hard candy, gum and some shiny new dines. Beside the tree was an apple crate full of apples, oranges, grapefruits, bananas and two fresh coconuts.

Mother liked her perfume and put some on right away so she would smell good all Christmas Day. Daddy put his pink socks on and he just laughed and laughed at his pretty pink feet. Most men don't like pink. It's Daddy's favorite color.

It was a great day. We ate off and on all day, anytime we wanted to. We played with all our stuff and listened to some more Christmas programs on the radio. Some told Christmas stories, and others just played Christmas songs. Mother and Daddy napped (off and on) all day. A good Christmas. A peaceful day.

December 30, 1954—Thursday

Bruce and I have awful colds. We wake up every morning with our eyes matted shut with yellow matter and keep trying to hock up thick green phlegm. Mother has to bathe our eyes with warm water before we can open them.

After we ate breakfast, Mother boiled a pan of water on the cook stove and put two tablespoons of Vicks Salve in it. It sure did stink up the house. Then she made each of us, one at time, hold our head over the rapidly boiling water, while she held a towel over our head, making a tent-like shape. We had to breathe the hot Vicks fumes deep into our lungs. It was terrible. The steam was so hot, it blistered our faces. Bruce just cried and cried. Mother said the steam would break up the congestion and help get rid of our colds. She saved the pan of Vicks water and when Daddy came in, he had to do the same. Daddy has a bad cold, too. That's one of the bad parts about winter. We always get a terrible cold or the flu and are sometimes sick for weeks.

1955

January 1, 1955—Saturday

Happy New Year! We didn't do anything special today. Just stayed home and goofed around. Mother made a chocolate mayonnaise cake with a double fudge frosting. I love mayonnaise cakes!   I don't understand how a cake can have mayonnaise in it that you can't taste.   Mother says it's a trick.

January 8, 1955—Saturday

Today was Bruce and Grandmother Reed's birthday. We went to her house for dinner, and they shared a birthday cake. Bruce is five and Grandmother is forty-seven.

January 14, 1955—Friday

I haven't written much about Jake. He is the old red mule Daddy plows the garden and fields with. This morning when Daddy went out to milk the cows, Jake was lying in the field. He was very sick. Mother and Daddy tried to get him up to bring him to the cow pen behind the smokehouse where the wind would be cut off him. But they couldn't get him up.

Daddy went to town and called the veterinarian from Mr. Randall's house. He told Daddy a long time ago that if we ever had an emergency and needed to use a phone, that we could use theirs. Mr. Blake, the vet, said he would be right out. He said it would take him about forty-five minutes to get to our house.

Mother covered Jake with an old blanket while Daddy was gone. When the veterinarian got there, he took one look at Jake and said he would be dead within an hour. He said Jake had pneumonia and there was nothing they could do for him. He suggested that Daddy shoot him to put him out of his misery, but Daddy said he just couldn't. He loved old Jake so much. Daddy didn't have long to worry, because Jake took a few more shallow breaths, then he was gone. Daddy was glad. He said he couldn't have shot poor old Jake.

We had Jake's funeral and buried him in the edge of the woods next to where Snowball was buried. Daddy had to dig a really big hole for Jake, bigger than for a real person.

January 31, 1955—Monday

At supper tonight, Daddy said he wasn't going to get another plow horse. We won't be having as big of a garden as we always have. We aren't going to grow cotton, sweet potatoes or peanuts any more, and we won't plant anything in the fields across the road. We will have a smaller garden beside the house and grow just the food we need to eat. Daddy said he was going to buy one of those new hand plows they have been advertising in the *Farmer's Almanac*. It has a sharp blade, and you push it to till up the ground. The dirt in this garden spot is sandy loam and should be easy to till with the new tiller and a hoe. I think Daddy is afraid of getting attached to another animal, like he did Snowball and Jake, then having it die, too.

February 9, 1955—Wednesday

Tomorrow is "hog killing day". Daddy says hogs are killed on the coldest day of the year. I know tomorrow is supposed to be really cold, fourteen degrees, the weatherman on the radio said. We listen to the farm program on the radio every morning during breakfast. Snow has been on the ground for three days, so tomorrow will be the day. Mother says we have to go to bed early because we have to get up early. Bruce and I love to play in the snow. Yesterday we built a snowman. We put one of Daddy's old work caps on him and Mother gave us buttons for his eyes and nose. We put a stick in his mouth for a pipe, then Daddy cut a piece of corncob and, after having made a hole in it with his pocket knife, put it on the end of the stick. Yep, our snowman has a corncob pipe, for real.

After dinner, Mother made some snow ice cream. She just uses snow, vanilla flavoring, sugar, and cream from the top of the milk. Since we milk our own cows, we always have plenty of fresh cream. Mother made a big dishpan full of the ice cream and let us eat all we wanted. Bruce and Daddy put chocolate syrup on theirs, by not me! I liked it just the way it was.

February 10, 1955—Thursday

We got up at five o'clock this morning. Mother cooked us a big breakfast because she said we wouldn't get anything else to eat until the hog was slaughtered, dressed, and the meat had been packed in salt.

Daddy wouldn't let us come outside until the hog was slaughtered. He shot it in the head.

He says it's the quickest way. It was hard for him to kill it, after all, he raised that hog from a baby, petting and feeding it every day. He talks to the hog like it is a little kid. Then to think, we will be eating it! It's even hard for me. It's like eating your pet dog. I guess farm folks just get used to it.

First, Daddy got a hot fire going underneath the old black wash pot. When it was at a roaring boil, he shot the hog. Using a hoist he had made, he and Mother slowly raised the 250 pound hog by pulling him into the air with ropes. Daddy cut the hog's throat and let him bleed. That means they let all the blood drain out of him, so the meat won't be spoiled or tainted. They caught the blood in dishpans, then threw it over the fence. Some people put the blood in their sausage when they make it, but Mother said that we don't.

Then they slowly lowered the hog into the pot of boiling water. They used dippers to pour scalding water all over him as he was too big to fit into the pot.

When he was all scalded, they raised the hog higher into the air, so they could work with him. They scraped all the hair off the hog with butcher knives. Daddy cut the hog's belly wide open and cleaned out all his guts, intestines, heart, liver, stomach, you know, all that nasty stuff. They poured hot water all over his insides using the dippers, making sure he was clean and that all the blood was rinsed away. Daddy had already sharpened all Mother's butcher knives the day before getting them ready for the kill. It takes several awfully sharp knives to cut up a whole hog.

Mother and Daddy spent the whole day cutting up the hog and packing it into salt. It stays so cold in the smokehouse that it will not spoil. The salt will help preserve it. After a couple of weeks, they will take the meat with the salt still on it and hang the large pieces from wire that Daddy has attached to the rafters. He will build a very small smoldering fire on the dirt floor underneath the meat to smoke it. This preserves the meat more. He uses hickory wood as it gives the meat a good flavor.

Mother and Daddy will grind sausage tonight after supper. We have a hand-turned grinder that attaches to the edge of the kitchen cabinet. As Mother puts the pieces of pork that she has already seasoned into the grinder, Daddy will turn handle so that the meat comes out all chopped up, looking like real sausage. Then they will wrap it, ready for cooking. Tomorrow Mother will render some of the fat into lard and make lye soap from the rest.

After the hog was all ready to be "dressed" (a funny name for cutting up a hog isn't it?), we got to go out to the smokehouse and watch them work. Working with a hog's guts and blood sure smells bad! It makes me think that I won't be able to eat the meat.

The best part about hog killing day is suppertime. Mother always fries up a big platter of fresh pork. She rolls the sliced meat in milk and flour and fries it in the iron skillet. While a pan of biscuits cook in the cook stove, she makes a skillet of red-eye gravy from the meat drippings. In case you don't know what red-eye gravy is, you simply pour a cup or two of coffee into the grease and let it simmer. Then you divide a big biscuit in half and pour the gravy all over it until it is saturated. The fresh pork doesn't need any salt. The meat is salty enough naturally.

The bad part of hog killing day is how sick we always are for a day or two afterwards. Eating the fresh meat gives us all diarrhea, and do we really feel sick. This happens every year. You would think we wouldn't eat it again the next year, but we always do. All country folk and farmers do. Eating the fresh pork is such a special treat.

Now this part always made me go "Yek." Mother loves the hog innards! Her favorite part of the whole hog is the tongue. She likes both pig and cow's tongue. Isn't that awful? She boils it on the top of the stove for a long time, until it gets tender. It foams up and boils all over the stove. Boy, does it stink! She does this every year.

Another yekky thing Mother likes is squirrel brains. When Daddy kills a squirrel, she fries it up. While sitting at the supper table, she takes the handle of her table knife, and with one quick whack on the squirrel's skull, cracks it open. Then she digs out the brains with a spoon and mixes it with scrambled eggs. I don't know how she can eat a squirrel's brains, they are so puffy, like boiled liver. But she says they are delicious. I don't want to find out. She also likes tripe. That's the lining of a cow's stomach. Isn't that disgusting? Totally disgusting!

March 1, 1955—Tuesday

Old Bossie had a baby calf before daylight this morning. When Daddy went out to milk, there it was. It's so cute. It's black and white with a white nose. Bruce petted it then asked Daddy if he could bring it in the house. Daddy just laughed.

"No," he said. "But you can pet it any time your mother or I are out here. Don't come out here when no one is with you. The mother cow may butt you and she could even hurt you. She wouldn't mean to, of course, but that calf is her baby, and she will defend him."

Daddy said Bruce could name the calf. Bruce said he wanted to name him "Spot" because he has spots on him.

"Good name!" Daddy told Bruce, as he patted him on the head, then ruffled his hair. Daddy always ruffles our hair when he is in a good mood. No wonder I always look windblown.

March 12, 1955—Saturday

After Daddy got in from work, we went to see a lady called Mrs. Thompson. She had put a notice in the grocery store advertising that she wanted to sell her piano. Since I loved Grandmother Coppedge's piano so much, Mother and Daddy said they wanted to get one for me and give me piano lessons. Mrs. Thompson's husband brought the piano to our house in his pickup truck and he, Mother, Daddy, and Granddaddy Coppedge unloaded it and put it in the dinning room. I am so excited. We don't have any place else to put it except in the dining room, although it looks okay there.

March 13, 1955—Sunday

Mother went by Mrs. Carson's house this afternoon. She is an elderly lady who teaches piano lessons to all the kids in Ore City. Mrs. Carson said I could come at 7:15 every Monday morning for a thirty minute lesson, then walk the two blocks on to school. She said the lessons would be $5 a month, for the four lessons. I'm a little scared, but I sure do want to learn how to play like Grandmother Coppedge. Grandmother would love to teach me to play, I know, but Mother wants a professional to teach me.

March 15, 1955—Tuesday

Well, my first piano lesson is over. Mrs. Carson is very stern. She never smiled the whole time I was there. She said I have to practice an hour every day. I don't know enough stuff to practice a whole hour. Even so, Mother says that if she and Daddy are going to pay for the lessons, I will practice one hour! Sounds boring to me.

March 29, 1955—Tuesday

I've now had three piano lessons with Mrs. Carson. I don't think I'm cut out to be a piano player. The lessons make me real nervous, and I worry all week about the next lesson. She said I wasn't practicing enough. I still don't know enough to practice. Maybe it will get better. Grandmother Coppedge says she never took any dumb old lessons. She plays "by ear." That means she taught herself to play by just what sounds right. She sings a song and then picks out the notes to be the same sound as the song.

Maybe I should just learn to play by ear. That wouldn't cost anything; I wouldn't have to go to bed every night worrying about not practicing enough, and wouldn't have to go to Mrs. Carson's house again. She made her garage into what she calls her piano studio, and there is no heat in the room. It's cold in there and that makes me even more nervous, not to mention that Mrs. Carson still hasn't smiled even once.

March 30, 1955—Wednesday

Mr. Jackson, an elderly colored man who lives down the road, came by our house last night. He told Daddy that he had a new litter of baby pigs and wanted to give us one. He reminded Daddy of the morning last fall when Daddy stopped and helped him change a flat tire on his truck. He didn't have a spare so Daddy took him to the garage where he works, fixed the tire, then took him back to his truck and helped him put it on. Mr. Jackson has some kind of disease that makes him shake real bad. Daddy said it was hard for him to change the tire, and it made him feel good to help. Mr. Jackson wanted to repay the favor.

Mr. Jackson and his wife are raising four of their grandchildren. Their parents were killed in a bad train wreck two years ago. The train conductor said the kid's daddy pulled out in front of the speeding train despite him blowing the horn. There wasn't anything left of the car or them either. The train dragged their car a long way down the track. Luckily the kids had stayed with their grandparents for the weekend. The wreck happened on a Saturday night. The kid's mother and daddy were going to the dancehall across Sabine River.

Daddy told Mr. Jackson that he would come get the pig this Sunday.

April 1, 1955—Friday

This afternoon after school, Daddy let me go to Nelson's Grocery with him. While we were there, my cousin Debra Kay drove up in a fine green convertible, a tiny little car. She asked me if I wanted to go for a ride. Daddy said I could, but to be careful. Debra Kay and I rode around town then went on some long country roads where she could drive faster. What a thrill! She is only sixteen, and so pretty. How lucky she is to have a car. Her dad, my Uncle Raymond, owns the garage in town where Daddy works and everyone has their cars repaired. So, I guess that's how they can afford to buy her such a pretty car. I am still so excited, I may not be able to sleep tonight. I can still hear the sweet hum of the engine. I can only imagine how excited she must be. Everyone in town saw us. and they all had to come over and take a look at her car. I hope I can have my very own car someday.

April 10, 1955—Sunday

You just won't believe what happened this morning! About noon, Daddy let Bruce and me go with him to get the baby pig. Mother stayed home to rest. Mr. Jackson met us out in his front yard when we drove up. He and Daddy laughed and talked for a long time. We played with his grandchildren, but we were eager to see the baby pigs. They were way out in front of their farmhouse in the edge of the woods.

After a while, around noon, Daddy called Bruce and me to go to the pig pen. Mr. Jackson warned us to be careful and not get too close. He said the mama pig was very protective and wouldn't let anyone near her babies. I know Daddy must have heard what Mr. Jackson said, but he climbed over into the pen anyway. He reached down and picked up the baby pig he wanted, and just as he turned to walk over to the fence, the old mama pig clamped down on the toe of his shoe. All the pigs were squealing, and the mama was jerking her big head from side to side, tearing at Daddy's foot.

Mr. Jackson was screaming "Mr. Barney! Get out of that pen! Get out of that pen!" Daddy did a quick jerk with his leg; the pig lost her balance and fell in the mud. Daddy quickly stepped over the fence to safety, still holding the pig under his arm. Mr. Jackson was so upset, and got down on his knees to see how bad Daddy's foot was hurt.

"Oh, I'm all right", Daddy said with embarrassment.

"No, Mr. Barney. Look at all that blood. You're not all right. You're hurt! The end of your shoe is gone. That pig bit it off! Take your shoe off, Mr. Barney!"

Daddy handed the squealing pig to Mr. Jackson and sat down on a tree stump. He took off his shoe and ever so gently eased the sock off his bleeding foot. Then he just sat and stared at his foot. Half of his little toe on his right foot was gone. The pig had bitten it off, bone and all! Daddy didn't know what to do. At first it hadn't hurt, but then it was beginning to throb. And so much blood!

Mr. Jackson ran to the house screaming for his wife to get a pan of water and some clean rags. She quickly arrived with scissors, soft strips of white material from old worn out sheets, and a pan of water from the well. She cleaned and wrapped Daddy's foot real tight to try to stop the bleeding. Bruce and I were so scared. We hadn't said a word, only watched in panic.

After a while, Mr. Jackson helped Daddy to the car. He kept telling Daddy how sorry he was. "I'm just so sorry, Mr. Barney. I'm so sorry. Can I do anything else for you? Can I drive you home in my old truck?" Daddy said no, that he could make it. Besides, he needed to get the car home. Mr. Jackson put the pig in a wooden crate that Daddy had in the trunk. We got in and headed for home.

"Mother! Mother!" Bruce shouted as we got out of the car. "The pig bit Daddy! It bit half of his toe off! Come see, Mother! There is blood all in Daddy's shoe. Mrs. Jackson wrapped it up tight with rags, but it's still bleeding."

Mother helped Daddy into the house, led him to the bed, then put pillows under his leg to let gravity help stop the bleeding. She ran and got some aspirin for the pain, and put a cold rag on his head.

"Go get the pig out of the car," he told Mother. "It's in a wooden crate so it can't hurt you. Get Bruce Olen and Millie Jean to help you. Set the crate on their red wagon and pull it down to the pig pen. Put the crate in the pig pen, get out, and close the gate. Then use the broom handle to lift the door so he can get out and roam free.

"We'll get the crate out of the pen later," he told her. "The baby pig didn't bite me. The mama pig did. But the little one is so excited it might try."

The crate was heavy, but we managed to get it onto the wagon, and once we pulled it inside the pen, we sort of tilted the wagon back and let it slide off. We did as Daddy said and finally the pig was secure in his new pen. He was still excited and jittery and was running around in circles. He missed his mother and his sisters and brothers, I'm sure.

We went back to the house, and Daddy was just lying there. "I feel so stupid," he said. "Mr. Jackson warned me not to get too close to the mama pig. But

I've done that a thousand times and didn't think she would bother me. Boy, was I wrong. I feel bad for Mr. Jackson. In a few days, I'll drop by to reassure him that it wasn't his fault. I should have been more careful."

Daddy ate his dinner in bed so as to keep his foot and leg elevated, so it wouldn't start bleeding again. Mother let Bruce and me on the back porch.

April 11, 1955—Monday

I am writing this before the bus comes. Daddy must have dreamed about that pig biting him all night. I heard him crying out in his sleep, "Get out of the pen! Get out of the pen!" Mother said she was going to take him to the doctor today to have him take a look at Daddy's foot. So Daddy won't be going to work. Here comes my bus. Will write more tonight.

After Supper Same Day

The doctor said there was nothing he could do. There wasn't anything to sew up.

The end of the toe was just plain gone. It would just have to heal over, and would probably give Daddy trouble all his life. I don't really understand what that means, but Daddy is going back to work tomorrow. He went ahead and cut the entire end of his shoe out, so he can wear the bandage and it won't be too tight. The doctor told him that if it started to swell really bad to get off of it and go to bed, with pillows under his leg like Mother had done yesterday.

April 17, 1955—Sunday

Tonight we went to church with Aunt Sadie and Uncle Barry. We visited a Pentecostal church in Cedar Springs, about five miles from Ore City. My family is Baptist, and I had never been to a Pentecostal church. Wow! Are they different from us!

All we have in our church is a piano for music. At this church they have guitars, pianos, accordions, drums and symbols. They sing really loud and shout "Amen" after almost everything the preacher says. It sort of scared Bruce and me at first, but we got used to it.

Aunt Sadie goes to the Ore City Pentecostal Church, but she wanted us to visit this one with them. They were having a revival. A revival means that they will go to church every night for a week. This was the only night we are going. I liked the accordion music. Some day I might learn to play the accordion. Maybe it's easier than the piano.

The strangest thing they did was to wash each other's feet. I still don't understand why they did that. Everyone takes a bath and gets dressed up before they go to church, so why would their feet be dirty? Mother says it's a religious thing. She tried to explain it, but I didn't understand. She says that when I get older, I'll understand.

April 18, 1955—Monday

I am having to learn how to play the song "America" on the piano. I guess I'm doing all right, but I still don't like to practice. I just want to know how to play all at once, like magic. I guess Mrs. Carson is nice enough, but I just want to stop going. I worry all the time about her getting mad at me for not practicing enough.

April 25, 1955—Monday

Happy day! Happy day! I guess Mother and Daddy realized I just don't have the heart for learning to play the piano. They said that by the end of May when school is out, if I still don't want to take the piano lessons any more, I won't have to. We will stop them for the summer because I won't have a way to get there and get back home since we only have one car, and we just won't start them back in the fall when school starts. I can hardly wait! I think they probably think I will get to liking the lessons and Mrs. Carson better by then and not want to quit. But I won't. I want to quit today. Like I said, I'm just not cut out to be a piano player. I know Grandmother Coppedge will be sad and disappointed, but she loves me and she'll understand.

May 1, 1955—Sunday

Grandmother Reed took a bus to Albuquerque, New Mexico to help take care of her sister who is going to have surgery, so we didn't go to her house today for Sunday dinner. We always watch the colored folks who live down below us, walk to town all the time. Bruce and I beg Mother and Daddy to let us walk to town but they say that the two miles there and back is too far, especially for Bruce who is so little. But today, Daddy agreed that we would all walk to the graveyard and back. (Uppity folks call it the cemetery). A lot of our family is buried there and there are a lot of pretty flowers on the graves.

After a breakfast of pancakes and sausage, Bruce's favorite, we headed toward the road for our walk. We were so excited. Mother stopped us and gave us some rules for the walk: 1. Stay on the edge of the road, 2. Watch out for cars and log trucks (even though they don't usually run on Sunday), and 3. Don't get too far ahead of Mother and Daddy.

We passed Grandmother and Granddaddy Coppedge's house, went up the hill and around the curve. As we got in front of Mr. Cleeb's house, we saw him sitting on his front porch. He was in his straight-back cane chair leaning against this house, whittling.

Mr. Cleeb is about eighty years old. He is a very dark colored man, almost dark purple, and looks really scary, but is friendly and always waves at us when we pass in the car.

The tale has it that, when he was young, he fell in love and married a pretty, young colored woman from Harleton. After a while, their marriage went sour, and she started sneaking out of the house at night after they had gone to bed. Old timers say that she walked into the woods to meet a lover. Cleeb was hard of hearing from a disease he had when he was little, and a heavy sleeper, so he never knew she was gone. She was always back in bed before time for him to wake up.

One hot summer's night, Cleeb woke up thirsty and went out onto the back porch to draw water from the well. He saw her coming out of the woods. He hadn't noticed that she wasn't in bed because it was so dark in the house. They had a terrible argument. She ran into the house and got the shotgun that he kept in the bedroom beside the bed, aimed at him and fired. It hit him right in the face and blew part of his teeth and half his face off, leaving him terribly deformed looking.

She ran through the woods to the highway and flagged down a car and told them what had happened, then simply disappeared. No one ever saw her again.

Mr. Cleeb slowly recovered, but the town's folks say he was never "quite right" after that. His brains all got shot up.

Daddy called out a friendly hello to Mr. Cleeb, and he replied, "Looks like you folks got a good day for walking." They exchanged a few words then we went on our way, none too soon for me. Even though Mr. Cleeb is nice, he still scares me. Mother says that he doesn't have electricity, so when it gets dark, he just goes to bed.

Mr. Creeb never remarried and never had any children. He has no family left, especially since he is so old himself.

We went on down to the graveyard. Mother and Daddy walked through all the graves commenting on who was buried there, who was kin to whom, and, in general, remembering long-ago times. Bruce and I followed them for a while until we got bored hearing about dead people we didn't even know, then we started just looking around. We saw two rabbits just outside the graveyard fence and watched them play until they finally hopped off into the woods.

By the time we got back home, we were thirsty and ready for dinner. Mother had fixed fried chicken and made potato salad before breakfast, so we didn't have long to wait to eat. After dinner, we all laid down for a nap. We were all tired, but we had a wonderful day.

May 5, 1955—Thursday

We have been saving for a long time to buy a television set. We have a radio, but wow, a television! None of my friends have a television yet. Grandmother Reed's best friends have one, and sometimes we all go over to their house on Saturday night and watch the fights. I would rather play outside in the dark than watch the fights. We play chase and other games or sit on the back porch and tell scary stories. Bruce and I like to play by ourselves.

When Daddy gets in from work today, Bruce and I are going to get to go with him to Gilmer to buy the television. Mother says she wants to stay home and rest.

Oh, Daddy's toe is all healed up now. He limped around for several weeks. He still wears the shoe with the toe cut out because he says it swells sometimes when he has been standing a long time at work. He says it doesn't hurt much now. I'm glad.

Later that Night

What a scary ride home. It was just getting dark when we got to Gilmer. Daddy picked out the television he wanted, and one of the men in the store helped him load it into the front seat of the car. Daddy told me to sit in front and hold onto it in case he had to stop in a hurry. He told Bruce to sit in the back seat, but to jump up and help me hold it in case something happened. Daddy was nervous, afraid he would break it before he got it home.

By then, it was totally dark. About half way home, Daddy gasped and hit his breaks, but it was too late. A huge cow slammed into the front of the car. She was trying to run across the road. The impact threw her up on the hood and crashed into the windshield. The television slammed into the dash with no time for Bruce or me to react to try to catch it.

Daddy brought the car to a stop. The cow rolled off the hood, jumped to her feet and ran off into the darkness. Daddy was shaking all over, repeatedly asking if we were hurt. Once assured that we were all right, he inspected the television to see if it was broken. The television was not hurt, but our windshield was a cracked mess. After we all stopped shaking and calmed down, Daddy said, "Well, at least the television set is okay." We rode on home, marveling at what had happened.

May 7, 1955—Saturday

This evening, after work Daddy is going to take Bruce and me fishing at the creek just outside the city limits. Bruce and I have been digging worms all day. It's really hard to find any. It's so hot, they burrow deep into the hard ground looking for moisture. We got 10. We put them in an empty Pork-N-Bean can with a little dirt and grass. They are sitting under the back porch steps in the shade until Daddy gets home so they won't die. We each have a cane pole and it's already fixed with the line, a red and white bobber cork and a shinny gold hook. Granddaddy Reed says you must always have a sharp, new hook if you're going to catch anything, especially the big ones. Daddy has a sack with twenty-five gold hooks, all sizes. He bought them at Nelson's Store.

Later in the Day

Boy, are we tired! We caught seven sun perch. They aren't very big, but if Mother fries a big skillet of potatoes and makes some hot biscuits, they will be enough for supper.

When we got to the creek, we parked the car on the side of the road and walked back to a little pathway. We sat under the bridge most of the time. That's where the water is the deepest, and we were getting bites right off the bat, so no need to move. Anywhere along the creek bank is good, all under lots of shade trees. If you go too far, red bugs and ticks get pretty bad. Old Mr. Wheatley has some cows not far from there, and they come up to drink water out of the creek. Daddy says that's why ticks are pretty bad father on down.

Every time Daddy would get a nibble on his line, he would jerk his pole out of the water high into the air and just laugh and squeal "Got another one! Got another one!" We caught a lot, probably fifteen or twenty but some of them were too small and we had to throw some back.

After Supper

Man, were those fish good. Mother put an onion in the potatoes making what she calls country-fried skillet potatoes. She made a big pan of biscuits and let us have sorghum syrup as a treat. There's nothing like sweet warm syrup to sop up with buttery biscuits. I guess you'd say that was our desert.

Daddy was sad again after supper. We always saved the best scraps for Snowball. The rest went to the pigs. It was always Daddy's job to feed him. He just sat on the back porch steps in the dark. I watched him through the back screen door. He stared off into the woods like he thought Snowball might come running out to meet him. Poor Daddy.

May 20,1955—Friday

Today was the last day of school. I made a good report card and was passed to the third grade. I'll be in Mrs. Johnson's class next year. She is really strict and hardly ever smiles at anyone. I like her. She smiles at me and talks to me on the playground.

Ms. Beverley wrote on the bottom of my report card, "Millie Jean needs to work harder in reading and is careless in writing." Oh, well, I passed. That's all I care about. I'm so glad it is summer. I can sleep late and won't have to get up so early to catch that stinkin' old bus.

Daddy says a traveling roller rink is coming to Ore City next week and that we can go. I can hardly wait. Bruce and I have never been on a real roller rink floor.

Oh, I forgot. My very last piano lesson has come and gone! Hoorah! Hoorah! Now I won't have to worry any more, or practice any more, or have everyone telling me, "You're going to follow in your Grandmother's steps and grow up to be a great pianist." School is out, and all I want to do is play, play, play. And not the piano!

May 21, 1955—Saturday

Daddy got up before five o'clock this morning to clean out the chicken house. We are going to Gilmer to buy some baby chickens. Daddy said that this time we are going to get fifty. Last year we bought twenty-five, but the weather turned off cold suddenly, and many of them died. He said we would buy more this time and maybe more would survive. I love getting baby chicks. They peep all the way home and run around in the chicken pen peeping and digging in the dirt like they are looking for something, maybe a worm. I don't know. Maybe they just like to dig.

Just Before Dark

Well, we made it home with all the baby chicks. They are so sweet. Bruce sat and played with them all evening. He just giggles and giggles as the chicks peck him all over. He tries to kiss them and they peck him on the face, then he falls back in the grass and just laughs and laughs. Mother and Daddy say we have to be very careful and not play too rough with them, or we might injure them. Daddy is putting some low hanging light bulbs in the chicken house to keep them warm at night. He also is putting a big piece of ply board on the front to keep out the cold air. I wish school were still going on so I could tell al my friends about the chicks. I can still tell them when school starts. By then, they'll all be big.

April 12, 1955—Tuesday

Daddy brought home six rat traps this evening. I don't mean mouse traps. I mean rat traps. Every night when we go to bed, we can hear big rats playing in the loft. They sound like they are having a wild party, jumping from rafter to rafter and falling all over the place.

Daddy says they are so bad on our place because we live in the country and they feed on the cow and pig's feed stored in the smokehouse. They also gnaw on our ham and other cuts of pork hanging in the smokehouse. Daddy opened the smokehouse door several times lately and caught them munching away.

"Are we really going to have to eat the meat now that the rats have crawled all over it and eaten part of it away?" I asked Mother.

"Yes," she said. "Meat is too precious to throw away." She said that she would wash it good and cut off the parts where the rats had eaten. She assured me that, once the meat had been cooked in the hot skillet or in the oven, all the germs on it would be killed anyway.

Daddy let Bruce and me climb up into the loft, and we watched him set the traps. He put one on each end of the loft, 2 in the front of the house and 2 in the back. Bruce and I had never been in the loft before. It was a little scary. There were a lot of spider webs and about a bgillion rat droppings covering everything. It smelled musky and ratty, if you know what I mean.

Daddy wouldn't let us get too close when he actually set the traps. He said that if we tripped one, it could hurt us bad, maybe break our fingers or a hand. He laid a piece of sharp, golden cheese on the flap, then pulled the lever all the way back down until it caught underneath the catch. Daddy got awfully nervous when he set the traps. If the lever doesn't catch just right, the trap will throw right there in your hands.

We climbed down from the loft, then headed for the smokehouse where Daddy set two traps that Granddaddy Coppedge had given him. These traps were for really big rats, bigger than the ones in the house. He put one between the corn (cow feed) and the shorts (pig feed) bins, and the other one on the dirt floor under the meat. He said that maybe while the rats are eating on our big ole ham, they will smell the cheese and drop down for a little snack. Daddy said, "Boy! Won't they be surprised!"

April 13, 1955—Wednesday

Wow! We caught a lot of rats today. Daddy said he heard one of the traps in the loft throw during the night. He heard the rat flopping all over the place, and he couldn't go back to sleep for a long time until it quit flopping.

Before Daddy went to work this morning, he got the ladder and climbed up into the loft opening and looked around with the flashlight. He could see that all four traps had   rats in them, but he told us at breakfast that he wouldn't go up there and get them until after work this evening, when he got through milking. He said he didn't want to get all dirty and stinky before he went to work.

Late in the Evening

Mother had some pieces of cheese already cut and ready this evening when Daddy got home. He let Bruce and me climb back into the loft again and watch him take the rats out of the traps. He put them in a tow sack. All four were dead and all smashed up where the lever had slammed down on them. One even had blood and guts squashing out all over the place. They smelled so, so bad! Daddy gagged and made funny noises as he took each one out of the trap and dropped it into the sack. He reset the traps with the fresh cheese. We climbed down the ladder and headed for the smokehouse.

When Daddy opened the smokehouse door, he just stood there holding onto the door handle staring down at the sprung trap directly under the ham that was hanging from the ceiling. As Bruce and I pushed the door open wider so we could see inside, we froze. Lying smashed by the big trap was a rat as big as the yellow tabby cat that often strays into Grandmother Coppedge's back yard.

"Why, I've never seen such a huge rat!" Daddy said with a long sigh. "No wonder such big chunks of our ham are being eaten, and your mother's quilts stored on the shelves are chewed all to pieces. She even found a nest of baby rats last week in one of the quilts." Daddy said he was going to keep the traps set all the time, just in case more come onto our place out of the woods.

May 28, 1955—Saturday

Last night we went to the traveling roller rink. It is a skating rink on wheels like a trailer house only big and wide. It had a big wooden floor and a canvas top like at revival meetings. They rented shoe skates to us for ten cents a pair and sold popcorn and cokes. Mother and Daddy sat on the benches that were around the inside of the rink and watched everyone skate. Bruce and I quickly got more confidence, and, with such a wide open space, not like skating down the hall at home, we felt free to fly around the floor. We both fell a lot but had a great time. It closed at nine o'clock. Boy, were our legs tired. Bruce woke up crying during the night with charley horses in his legs. Daddy rubbed them until he went back to sleep. The man at the rink said he would be back the same time next year. I can hardly wait.

May 30, 1955—Saturday

Today, Tootsome, a colored man who lives down the road in one of the sawmill shotgun houses, stopped by to show us his new black, two-door Ford coupe. Tootsome is about forty years old and has never gotten married. He lives with his sister, works at the sawmill, and is the only one down there who has a car. Until now, the rest of the families had to walk everywhere they went. He had that car shinning so we could see ourselves in it. He told Daddy that if he ever had car trouble, he would gladly give him a ride. Everyone is so proud for Tootsome. He has saved a long time for that car. It is some fine looking car!

June 4, 1955—Saturday

Spending the whole day in Gilmer is such a treat. Mother washed and rolled her hair and mine before we went. All the women wear their hair rolled up when they go to town on Saturday. They use bobby pins to hold the curls in place and put a pretty scarf around their heads. That way their hair is pretty the next morning for church.

Mother said it was so hot that she wanted to stay in the cool stores all day. We ate those wonderful juicy hamburgers at Lovell's Café and got a real Coca Cola. Mother doesn't buy them at the grocery store. She says they're too expensive, so when we get one at Lovell's it's a real treat. Lovell's makes the best hamburgers in the country. You can smell them in the air when you drive into town, especially on Saturday. They are really busy with farm folks coming in to eat.

The main thing Mother and Daddy were shopping for was a window fan. We don't have any kind of fan at home, and it's already so hot we can hardly sleep at night. We just lie in bed and sweat. We bought a pretty, light blue fan.

We got home about three hours before dark, so Daddy said he was going to put the fan together and get it in the window before dark so we could sleep cooler. He sat the fan on the floor in the living room and was working on it. He had raised the window and was measuring the size of the opening.

"Yep, I think it will fit," he said. Once he had it together, he reached to plug it in to see if it was going to work before he put it in the window. He flipped the switch on, and it worked. Bruce was standing next to him holding onto Daddy's shoulder. His eyes lit up when the blade started turning and humming. The next thing we knew, he stuck his foot into the turning blades and screamed. Daddy grabbed him around the waist and jerked him back, but it was too late. Blood was going everywhere and the blades were slinging tiny red droplets. It had cut the tip of Bruce's big toe off, and was it ever bleeding. Daddy sure felt bad, but it wasn't his fault. Accidents just happen.

Isn't it ironic that Bruce Olen and Daddy both have the end of one of their toes cut off, and both on the right foot! But the accident only cut the tip of Bruce Olen's toe off, not as bad as Daddy's. Even though Bruce's bled a lot, there wasn't as much blood as Daddy's, either.

June 22, 1955—Wednesday

Early this morning, Daddy was on his way to the cow pen to milk the cows. He heard a funny noise and saw the grass ruffling in the high weeds between the cow shed and the toilet. He went on to the shed and got a shoved just in case it was a dangerous animal or snake. He eased back to the spot where the weeds had been moving. He could still hear the noise but couldn't quite place what it sounded like. As he slowly and softly stepped toward the spot, he startled a mother cottontail, and she darted into even higher weeds.

Still hearing the noise, he crept closer, and there in a soft nest lay eight tiny newborn baby rabbits. After admiring them for a few minutes, Daddy eased back the way he had come, careful not to disturb them. He went on and milked the cows, then called us into the kitchen when he got back into the house.

"Bruce and Millie Jean, guess what I found? A nest baby rabbits out behind the hill on the way to the cow shed. Before long, we'll have rabbits hopping all over the place! But you must not bother them. If you touch them, their mother will abandon them, and they'll die. Don't go near them until they start coming out of their nest." Daddy had the sweetest smile on his face. His eyes sparkled as he took a deep breath and poured the milk from the bucket into a gallon jug.

June 25, 1955—Saturday

Daddy sat the big black wash pot up at the edge of the yard next to the garden and collected wood to make a fire under it. When it was boiling, we killed ten of our old hens. Grandmother Reed got a freezer last week and she said we could put them in there. Then every Sunday when we go to her house for dinner, we can bring one home with us for the next week.

I hate chicken killing time. Mother and Daddy take each chicken by the head and ring them around in a circle in the air real fast. It breaks the chicken's neck. They throw the chickens aside on the ground, while continuing to break the other chicken's necks. Those on the ground flop around for a long time, before they finally calm down and die. It's an awful thing to watch. Then they dip each chicken into the boiling water in the pot, lifting it up and down for a few seconds. Holding the chicken in the air, they pull the feathers out of the chicken. That's called plucking the chicken. It's hard to do because their feathers are still so hot from the water.

Mother and Daddy hand Bruce and me each a chicken after most of the feathers have been plucked out. By this time they have cooled off. We finish plucking them and put them in big dishpans. When all ten were plucked, Mother and Daddy hold each chicken over the fire under the pot and singe the remaining fuzz from the chicken's bodies. It really stinks. I really, really hate killing the chickens that we play with all the time. They are like our friends. Daddy says that's part of farm life. Just like hog killing is.

After they are all singed, Mother takes them to the back porch. She stands on the ground using the porch as a table. It takes about an hour to "dress" the chickens. That means to cut off their heads, cut them open and clean out the guts, then wash and cut them up. She uses a big butcher knife that Daddy has sharpened really sharp, like with the hogs. Then, she wraps each chicken in white butcher paper and tapes up the ends, and puts them into a wooden box to take to Grandmother Reed's freezer.

Before Mother wraps the chickens, she cuts the feet off and puts them aside. One night for supper, she will fry them all up. I can hardly wait. She fries them real crispy, kinda like French fries. Along with hog's innards, pickled pig's feet, and tripe, Mother surely loves her fried chicken's feet!

It was dark by the time we got to Grandmother Reed's. We took the chickens to the freezer, then told Grandmother that we were all tired and had to get home. We told her we would see her next Sunday for dinner.

Oh, we use those stinky old feathers to make pillows and to stuff mattresses. They never stop stinking, no matter how long they are left in the hot sun to cure.

July 17, 1955—Sunday

Yesterday, something happened that will always stay in my mind until the day I die. About a week or so ago, a thirteen year old girl, a distant relative by marriage, got real sick and was put in the hospital. At first they thought she had some kind of flu or something, then they thought she had gotten into some poison, but they couldn't find out what.

Well, she died Thursday, and yesterday the funeral home brought her body out to her house. Grandmother Reed said that her body will stay there until the funeral. She said that is what they do when somebody dies. The funeral men set the coffin right there in the living room and all the family and friends come to the house to pay their respects to the family. They view the body, then sit around and talk and eat, then talk some more.

Now, here is the strange part. Tradition has it that the body cannot be left alone at all, even during the night while the family sleeps. Someone "sits up" with the dead person.

Grandmother and I sat up with the body from 8 P.M. until 11 P.M. last night so the mother and daddy of the little girl could get some sleep. Three whole hours of just sitting and staring at a dead girl!

Well, Grandmother had to go to the bathroom, so she told me to sit right by the coffin until she got back. Holly terror! I was scared out of my bejebas! The room was only lit by a small table lamp in the corner. As I looked at the girl's face, I expected her to turn to me and say, "What are you staring at?" I was totally petrified. My chair was about twelve inches away from the end of the coffin, so I moved it to the other end so I couldn't see her face.

Then, that was even worse. I thought I could see her chest going up and down as she breathed, and once I even saw her hand move. What if she reached over and caught the side of the coffin, raised up and said, "Where am I?" Holly Cow!

"Hurry up, Grandmother," I whispered under my breath. "What's taking you so long?" I swear I could hear the dead girl breathing. It was deathly quiet in that house. I wondered if she knew I was sitting there. I wondered if she knew she was dead. I had never touched a dead person before, but I wasn't about to touch her. She might just raise up and say, "Just what do you think you're doing? Get your hands off me!"

I heard the bathroom door squeak and the light switch click off, not any too soon either.

"Are you all right, Millie Jean?" Grandmother asked as she stepped back into the light. "Everything okay?"

"Yea, Grandmother. Everything's fine," I lied.

Monday the funeral home people will come in a hearse and pick up the girl and take her to the church for he funeral services. It's a lot like a church service. The preacher says some really nice things about the dead person, preaches a little sermon about heaven and hell, then everyone in the church walks by the coffin and takes one last look at the dead person and says their good-byes.

Then, they all get in their cars, while the body is loaded into the hearse again for the last time, and they all drive to the graveyard real slow with the hearse leading the way. The close family members ride in a fancy new funeral home car, just behind the hearse. No one can ride in the hearse except the driver and the preacher.

Then once they get to the burial site, a nice canopy is already set up over the hole that has been dug for the coffin. About fifteen metal chairs are sitting on a rug. This is where the parents, siblings, Grandparents and other close family members sit, while the preacher gives another short sermon, saying how this person's soul has now gone to heaven to be with God. Then the preacher goes down the row and shakes the hands of all those sitting down, then mingles in the crowd shaking other people's hands. Everyone stands around talking and crying. Eventually everyone goes home. Some go back to the dead person's house, eat and talk until everyone is plum tuckered out, and then go home.

I hope the next time someone dies, we can just go to visit and won't have to sit up again. I will probably have nightmares for months over this affair.

July 30, 1955—Saturday

I haven't written in my diary since a really awful thing happened last Sunday. A family that is distant kin to Daddy came to eat Sunday dinner with us and spend the afternoon. Their names were Clisco and Maude Mae. They had two kids the same age as Bruce and me.

After dinner, the four of us kids played outside while the adults sat around and talked. We had a great day, until the end. Mother and Daddy were walking them out to their car to tell them good-bye when Bruce started crying, asking for a drink of water. He had asked Mother and Daddy, but they told him to wait a few minutes until the company was gone, then they would get him one.

Bruce said there was some water on Mother's quilting frame where she had been quilting for the last two weeks and asked me to please give him a drink. It was July and we had been playing out in the hot sun. Bruce was red in the face and really thirsty, so I told him all right, and we went into the back room where the quilting frame was. I reached on my tip toes and got the quart of water. The lid was on tight, so I used the tail of my dress as I had seen Mother and Grandmother Reed do so many times and unscrewed the lid.

Bruce guzzled down the water, quenching his thirst. The next thing I remember, Mother and Daddy were racing us to the car. They threw me in the back seat; Mother put Bruce in her lap in the front, and Daddy slammed the car into back-up gear and tore out of the driveway, leaving red dirt flying everywhere. He almost lost control of the car as he flew out onto the road. I couldn't see over the seat and didn't understand why we were driving so fast. Daddy started blowing the car horn continually. Beep! Beep! Beep! Beep!

Suddenly our car swerved over to the side of the road. Mother jumped out with Bruce still in her arms, and Daddy dragged me out of the back seat. We ran to Clisto's car. They had heard our horn blowing and pulled off the road. Daddy explained that Bruce had drunk coal oil and we had to get to the hospital and fast. Daddy was too shook up to drive our car and knew that Clisco's car would go faster.

I still didn't understand why everyone was so upset. Bruce only drank the water from the fruit jar. Mother and Daddy drink water from a fruit jar all the time and it doesn't make them sick. Why would it make Bruce sick?

Everyone cried and prayed all the way to the hospital. They were talking about Bruce dying. Then I really got scared. They were talking about how "Millie Jean had given him the coal oil to drink, and he may die!" Were they saying that I had poisoned him?

Once we were at the hospital, Mother ran in with Bruce in her arms screaming that her baby had drunk coal oil. The nurse grabbed him in her arms and ran into a back room with him. She shouted for everyone to wait outside. Another nurse came out and asked how long it had been since he drank it and how much did he drink.

Everyone was comforting Mother and Daddy and treating me like I had done something horribly wrong. I guess I must have, but I didn't mean to. I only meant to give Bruce a drink of water. No one would talk to me.

It was dark before we left Ragland's Clinic. By the time Clisco got us back to our car and we drove on home, everyone was exhausted and we went straight to bed.

The next day, I was told how the doctor had to run a tube down Bruce's throat and pump the coal oil out, and how he almost died, because I gave it to him to drink! They said the effects of the fuel would probably stunt his growth, meaning he would not grow much bigger. I guess I will always be blamed for what happened. But it was an accident. I'll never understand why coal oil was in the water jar.

August 1, 1955—Monday

Bruce is finally doing better. He had a terrible sore throat yesterday, and slept most of the day. Daddy said it was caused from all the stuff they did to him in the emergency room at the hospital. Everyone is still mad at me and that's all they talk about. I just want to go crawl up under the house and go to sleep. Forever! Why do things like this always happen to me?

August 28, 1955—Sunday

We didn't go to Grandmother Reed's for the day like we often do on Sunday. Instead, we left Friday night after Daddy got off work and went to Dallas. We spent the weekend with Aunt Zelma, Uncle Jim and their two kids, June and Jimmy. Aunt Zelma made a good breakfast with homemade biscuits. Mother makes biscuits at home, but these were tiny, crispy biscuits. They tasted like they were made out of pie crust. Bruce and I put strawberry jam on them. I ate four and Bruce ate three. But that was all right. Aunt Zelma made a lot. There were even some left over. She said that if we got hungry during the day, we could have them with some of the blackberry jam that she made last week.

We went to the zoo on Saturday, then visited a lot of relatives on Sunday. Just before dark, we headed for home. It was late when we pulled into our driveway. I wish I could stay with Aunt Zelma someday. I bet she never wanted to be a farmer!

September 3, 1955—Saturday

Mother and Daddy have been picking cotton since Monday. Today we picked cotton all day, and are we tired. Bruce and I didn't pick much. We just played in the sand mostly. Picking cotton makes your hands bleed and sore. Mother and Daddy started picking about daylight while it was still cool. Bruce and I slept until way up in the morning then went across the road to the field where they were.

Bruce and I don't wear shoes during the summer, so the hot sand burns our feet when the day's sun gets really hot. When the sandy dirt gets too hot for us to stand, Bruce rides on the end of Mother's cotton sack and I ride on the back of Daddy's. Daddy pulls me because I am heavier. They don't really let us ride long because it makes them tired, but they do it for fun, then send us back across the road to the house to play. Daddy will take most of the cotton to the gin. Mother will use some of it to make quilts.

September 4, 1955—Sunday

We're not going to spend the day at Grandmother Reed's again today. Mother said since we went to see Daddy's oldest sister, we should go today to see Aunt Mildred, his youngest sister. She, Uncle Audrey and their son Ralph live in Union Ridge, not too far from here. We're going after breakfast.

The End of the Day

Bruce and I had a great time playing at Aunt Mildred's house. They live in the country, too. The best part is that Ralph has a little pond he calls "crawdad pond" that he built. It's way down in the pasture. He has tiny baby catfish, perch and brim, along with the crawdads. He keeps the crawdads in a separate part of the pond all by themselves. He built a bridge to walk over the pond. The whole pond is about the size of a car. It is about three or four feet deep. We played down there all day except for dinner time. Bruce and I got chiggers. I guess Ralph knows how to avoid them. Next time we'll ask him how so we won't go home all itchy.

September 14, 1955—Wednesday

Mr. Cleeb died today. Well, really a few days ago, I guess. One of the pulpwood truck drivers who waves at Mr. Cleeb every day when he passes, noticed him leaning against the house in his chair like he always does. He waved at him, but it appeared that Mr. Cleeb was asleep. After the third day, when Mr. Cleeb didn't wave, he pulled his truck over to the side of the road and got out. When he got to the porch, he could see that Mr. Cleeb was dead. Everyone says he went peaceful, in his sleep. He was a sad, lonely man. Maybe now he is happy in heaven, some folks say.

September 25, 1955—Sunday

This morning I woke up with a fat lip so big I could hardly see my nose in the mirror. Yesterday, Bruce and I went with Mother to Mrs. Higginbotham's house for what the ladies call a Home Demonstration Party. I don't know much about it. The important thing is that all the lady's kids get to come, and we play outside until refreshments are served. Then they bring out cookies and punch on the porch for us to eat.

Well, Catherine and Nancy were in the porch swing and I was pushing them. Elliott came from around the back of the house and jumped up on the side of the porch. When the swing came back toward him, he caught it and held it up in the air. The girls were squealing for him to let go. As I took a step forward to try to get the swing and help them, he suddenly let it go, and it hit me right in the face!

Boy, there was blood everywhere and all the kids started screaming. The women all ran outside and someone yelled for Mrs. Higginbotham to get some rags, for all the blood. The party got cut short because we had to leave for the hospital. Yep, Ragland's Clinic again! It's called a clinic, but it is doctor's offices combined with a hospital. Believe me, I do not want to see that place again! Ever!

All the way to the hospital, Mother kept talking about the doctor having to sew me up. That really scared me, but then, I couldn't see how bad I was hurt with all the rags wrapped round and round my face and head. All I could see was that blood was still dripping onto my new blouse.

As it turned out, my lip had been totally cut away from my face from the right side of my nose to the left side. Mother said it hung down, and she could see my teeth through the hole. The doctor said that he did not want to sew it up. He bandaged it in a special way and said to let it heal naturally. He said there would far less scaring without the stitches.

It hurt so bad when I woke up this morning that all I could eat was chicken broth and melted ice cream through a straw. Mother dipped the straw into the broth, held her finger over the end to keep the juice inside, then gently slipped it into my mouth and let go of the other end. The broth ran down my throat. The doctor said we didn't need to come back to see him unless it got infected. I still haven't seen it yet. The bandage has to stay on for three days before it can be taken off. I certainly hope this is our last visit to Ragland's Clinic.

October 4, 1955—Tuesday

My birthday! I'm 9 years old!!

Guess what happened today? When Daddy drove in the driveway and pulled up to the old board he keeps as a stopping point for the front tires, he didn't get out of the car. He just sat there for the longest time. Mother watched him out the front kitchen window. "Millie Jean," she called. "Go out and see what's wrong with your Daddy. He's just sitting in the car. Maybe he's sick. Go see."

As I ran down the back steps and headed around to the driver's side of the car, Daddy was sitting there with his head down. I was afraid something was bad wrong.

"Daddy," I said slowly, easing up onto the running board. "Is something wrong?"

"No, not much," he said, trying to hold his excitement, trying not to smile. He leaned forward and when he sat back up, he had a brand new puppy in his lap. A slow grin spread across his face as he waited to see my reaction.

"Oh, Daddy," I screamed as I took the fluffy ball of fur into my arms. "Bruce Olen! Come see what Daddy brought home. A puppy! It's a new puppy!" Trying to carefully run across the yard toward Bruce, who was playing in our playhouse out back, I held onto the flopping puppy in my arms. Mother came out onto the porch, and we all sat on the steps and played with our new puppy.

"I think we should name him Blackie," Daddy said, "since he is all black,"

"Then Blackie it is," Mother said. After our hearts had stopped pounding and things calmed down, Daddy said, "Millie Jean, go look under the front seat of the car, under the driver's seat."

Excitedly, I ran and flung the door open and bent down to search under the seat. "Oh, Daddy! I can't believe it. A new diary! How did you know that mine was almost full and I needed another one?"

"Well, you write in that thing all the time, and I knew that before long it had to be filled up. Ms. Minnie has them in her variety store in town. When I stopped in to give her your mother's crochet to sell, I saw them laying on the front counter. Since you already had a blue one, I got the pink one. That way you can tell which is which."

I can't believe it. Two wonderful surprises in one day! A new puppy **and** a new diary!